The Rise of Anime and Manga

UNDERSTANDING MANGA

From Fox Spirits to Fashion Icons

MARI BOLTE

TWENTY-FIRST CENTURY BOOKS / MINNEAPOLIS

To all the readers who are just discovering manga for the first time, and to those who have been here all along

Twenty-First Century Books™
An imprint of Lerner Publishing Group, Inc.
241 First Avenue North
Minneapolis, MN 55401 USA

For reading levels and more information, look up this title at www.lernerbooks.com.

Main body text set in Bembo Std Regular.
Typeface provided by Monotype Typography.

Library of Congress Cataloging-in-Publication Data

Names: Bolte, Mari author
Title: *Understanding manga : from fox spirits to fashion icons* / Mari Bolte.
Description: Minneapolis, MN : Twenty-First Century Books, 2026. | Series: The rise of anime and manga | Includes bibliographical references and index. | Audience: Ages 11–18. | Audience: Grades 7–9. | Summary: "One Piece and Naruto are two iconic manga series, but these are far from the only ones available. From other popular series to manga's influence worldwide, discover what manga is and its progression through history"—Provided by publisher.
Identifiers: LCCN 2025011256 (print) | LCCN 2025011257 (ebook) | ISBN 9798765662748 library binding | ISBN 9798348029647 paperback | ISBN 9798348000400 epub
Subjects: LCSH: Manga (Comic books)—History and criticism—Juvenile literature | LCGFT: Comics criticism
Classification: LCC PN8291 .B65 2026 (print) | LCC PN8291 (ebook) | DDC 741.5/952—dc23/eng/20250507

LC record available at https://lccn.loc.gov/2025011256
LC ebook record available at https://lccn.loc.gov/2025011257

Manufactured in the United States of America
1 – CG – 12/15/25

CONTENTS

INTRODUCTION

You're at your favorite bookstore and find yourself in the manga section. Tidy rows of books with color-coordinated spines line the shelves. You pick one up and look at the characters on the cover. The art looks interesting, so you flip the book open. But something seems odd. The story doesn't make sense. Finally, you remember. Manga is read back to front and right to left, not front to back and left to right. At first, it feels funny to be reading "backward." But the story is too good, and soon you're too drawn in to remember anything but what you just read.

People have been enjoying mass-produced illustrated books called *Ehon musha* in Japan since the early 1700s. Manga as we know it came into being over the next century, and modern books are heavily influenced by those early works.

The manga market has exploded in recent years. It reached sales of more than $14 billion in 2024 and is expected to surpass $22 billion by 2031. New fans are discovering manga every day. In 2021, first volumes of long-running,

Manga can be found anywhere books are sold, borrowed, or rented.

established manga such as *My Hero Academia*, *Attack on Titan*, and *Demon Slayer: Kimetsu no Yaiba* sold more than 160,000 hard copies each in North America—and that doesn't account for digital copies, subscription versions, library check-outs, or sales at comic book shops. "In the past year alone, we sold 200 percent more copies of *Persona 3, Vol. 1* than we did over the past seven years combined," Erik Ko, a Canadian manga publisher, said in 2022. The manga he referenced had originally been published in 2016. "It's almost like people didn't know that this manga existed until now!"

People might not have known manga was out there before. But they do now! Manga is more than comic books or cartoons. Dive in and get a deeper understanding of manga—and why it has captured the love of readers around the world.

CHAPTER ONE

What Is Manga?

Manga is an illustrated story. Most manga use speech bubbles and illustrated sound effects to tell the story, although there are also manga that don't use any words at all. The stories can be about anything, from heroes and villains to monsters and magic, or even regular people just getting through the day.

Traditional Japanese is read from right to left, and manga is as well. Some may think that this causes confusion for non-Japanese readers. But the opposite is true! Learning to read while following along with pictures and pairing the actions with sound effects engages the brain. It gives the brain multiple ways to take in the information. This is called multimodal learning. Manga also introduces different cultures and ideas in a clear way. Instead of imagining or relying on the author's description, readers can actually see what objects or settings look like. This is especially helpful if the manga is based on historical events or real people.

Mangaka use both ink and paper and digital tools to create manga. Both have their benefits.

The Makers: Mangaka

Manga creators, called *mangaka*, are often both the author and the illustrator. Being a mangaka is hard work. Anyone can do it, but not everyone can do it as a career. To get their

Eiichiro Oda was nineteen years old when he came up with the idea for *ONE PIECE*.

start in the industry, mangaka must be discovered by editors or publishers. They can do that by entering contests in magazines with short one-shot stories called *yomikiri*. *ONE PIECE*'s author Eiichiro Oda was only seventeen when he sold his first one-shot. Conversely, creator Kakusai Han grew up wanting to be a mangaka but didn't attract an editor until he turned sixty. In 2023, he published *67-sai no Shinjin: Han Kakusai Tanpenshu*, or *The 67-Year-Old Newcomer: A Collection of Short Stories by Kakusai Han*.

Once mangaka have been "discovered," they sign a deal for serialization. This means that their story will be published regularly, usually either weekly or monthly. And now the hard work begins. Having enough finished work to publish can be hard. Planning the story in advance takes time. Then it must be storyboarded and pencil sketched before finally being inked. "Many weekly manga artists work for a week with one day off," mangaka Nao Yazawa said. "There may be three days dedicated to story creation, one day for writing it, one day for pencil drawing, and then one day spent on inking it."

The manga also must be popular with fans. Manga magazines have voting cards inside. Readers vote for their favorite manga, and the magazine publishes the results. If a manga is consistently at the bottom, it can get canceled. Fans who like the manga may never see a finished story, and the mangaka will have to start all over from the beginning on something new.

DIY Drawings

Not every mangaka works with a big publisher. Some people self-publish. These works are called *doujinshi*. Doujinshi have been around since 1885, when *Garakuta Bunko* was first published with the goal of sharing the works of like-minded creators. Much like a modern zine, doujinshi were a way for mostly young people to express how they saw the world. They were also used as a political tool.

Meanings in Manga

Kanji, a Japanese writing system, was developed thousands of years ago. Japanese people borrowed from the Chinese writing system called *hanzi*, which uses thousands of symbols, or characters. Each character is unique and has its own pronunciation and meaning. Although some hanzi and kanji words may look similar—or even the same—pronunciations

Both Chinese and Japanese characters have evolved over time.

can be very different. Other characters have changed or evolved over time to mean different things. Think about languages other than English that use Roman letters. For example, the Spanish word *largo* looks similar to the English word *large*. But *largo* means "long," not "big."

Japanese was traditionally written in tall columns from top to bottom and right to left. This style was called *tategaki*. Influence from the Western world has changed Japan's writing system. Now, many Japanese texts are written left to right. This style is called *yokogaki*. It became popular after World War II (1939–1945). Today, only more traditional things, such as formal letters—and manga!—use tategaki.

A simplified version of kanji, known as *kana*, is often used for sound effects in manga. A kanji sound might take a dozen pen or brush strokes to draw. The same sound in kana might only take three or four. Kana groups consonants with vowels, such as *ka*, *ki*, *ku*, and so on. Kana can also be used to represent feelings or imagined sounds. When used in this way, it's called *gitaigo*. Examples of gitaigo used to convey meaning include when a character feels dizzy or experiences a sharp pain, stares at another character, or feels glum.

Modern doujinshi are a way for amateur mangaka to share their work and learn the process. Less than 10 percent of doujinshi authors do it as a full-time job. Self-publishing also allows mangaka to work on stories without the strict schedule forced by a mainstream manga magazine. Some publish fan fiction manga inspired by their favorite series. Anyone can create or sell doujinshi. A group of creators working together to publish a doujinshi—or just a single creator who puts out a doujinshi by themselves—is called a circle.

The most popular place to buy and sell doujinshi is at Comiket, also known as Comic Market. This convention dates back to 1975. In the 1980s, it grew with the rise of fan fiction and cosplay. Every year, more people attended. In 2019, more than 700,000 people and more than 30,000 circles went to the convention, along with between 20,000 and 30,000 cosplayers. They came from at least seventy-five countries, although exhibitors had to have a Japanese address. Numbers dropped after the COVID-19 pandemic by design with maximum restrictions of 55,000 attendees per day, but they are slowly climbing back to where they were. Japan lifted all COVID-19 restrictions in 2022, and by 2024, there were 260,000 attendees over two days.

Buying and Selling

Manga can be published and sold in several different ways. Manga magazines, such as *Super Jump* and *Weekly Shonen Sunday*, publish serialized stories. They come out every week or month, with single manga chapters of multiple series in each issue. *Nakayoshi* is a monthly magazine that has been

Comiket is the largest fan convention in the world and includes a winter and summer market.

published since 1954, making it the longest-running manga magazine. The best-selling is *Weekly Shonen Jump*, with an average weekly circulation of 1.28 million copies. Since its

In the United States, manga usually comes in two sizes. But in Japan, the sizes are much more varied.

launch in 1968, it has sold more than 7.5 billion copies.

Paperback books called *tankobon*, which are roughly 5 inches (13 cm) by 7 inches (18 cm), are popular. They can be purchased in bookstores, convenience stores, and even vending machines. Each volume contains about twelve chapters of a single story. In 2024, the longest manga of all time was a seinen manga that spanned 212 volumes and 975 chapters. Its first chapter was published in 1968.

In 2023, manga made up more than 40 percent of all publications sold in Japan. Its digital presence is even bigger. In 2023, $3.3 billion in manga was bought digitally, making up 90 percent of the digital publishing market. People buy e-books and get subscriptions to comic- or manga-reading apps where they can read from tablets, laptops, or even their phones. Manga is everywhere, and it's only getting more popular.

Lending Libraries

Publishing in Japan has been around for a long time. The oldest work printed in Japan dates back to sometime between 764 and 770 CE. For a long time, books were mainly for wealthy people and scholars. Around the 1700s, printers developed ways to make mass production easier. This meant that more books could be printed and more people could read them. In the 1800s, book lenders called *kashihonya* started renting books, or *kashihon*, to people for less than it cost to buy them. Manga outside of the general appeal of shonen (for young boys) and shojo (for young girls), such as horror or political stories, were especially popular. Like modern library books, kashihon were heavily stitched and held together with reinforced binding.

By the 1960s, kashihon began to decline. Manga magazines were becoming more widespread and affordable. There was no need to rent when they could be bought with pocket money.

CHAPTER TWO

Who Writes It?

Between serialized, self-published, and undiscovered creators, there are thousands of mangaka in Japan. Choosing life as a manga artist can be hard. Aspiring artists must work to get discovered. They may have to work day jobs to pay their bills. Serialized artists must constantly produce new content. The industry is famous for being physically and mentally demanding. Having to make new, high-quality content every week is draining. But if a mangaka does make it big, fame and fortune follow. Their stories are read around the world and are turned into anime, video games, novels, and even feature-length movies. For many, this is worth the price.

When mangaka take time off, it is a big deal. In 2024, *ONE PIECE*'s creator Eiichiro Oda, the wealthiest mangaka with a net worth of more than $200 million, took three weeks off. He needed to figure out the future of *ONE PIECE*. His mentor, Akira Toriyama, had recently passed away as well. Every time Oda takes a break, it is newsworthy. People immediately question his decision. But mangaka tend

Osamu Tezuka graduated with a medical degree from Osaka University, but he never ended up practicing medicine. Instead, he went on to create manga.

to live shorter lives than the average person, and people place the blame on their grueling schedules. Legendary mangaka Osamu Tezuka and Shotaro Ishinomori both passed away at the age of sixty. In contrast, Shigeru Mizuki, who created *GeGeGe no Kitaro*, lived to be ninety-three. He was famous for sleeping eight to ten hours a day. "Tezuka was always working through the night, and he died young," Mizuki said. "I've spent my life half-asleep, and I've lived a long time."

AI Manga

In March 2023, the first manga made using artificial intelligence (AI), *Cyberpunk: Peach John*, was released by publishing house Shinchosha. The author, Rootport, came up with the story's plot and character dialogue. But he had never drawn a comic of any kind. Instead, he used Midjourney, an online AI image generator that created pictures using user-input descriptions. It took just six weeks to create the full-color, hundred-plus-page manga.

The process wasn't seamless. AI notoriously has problems with drawing human hands. Rootport made sure to limit scenes with hands. The image generator also could not recreate the same characters from panel to panel, which meant that distinctive details—such as clothing colors or hairstyles—had to be used to help readers figure out which characters were which.

The ethics of using AI are still being debated. Many artists feel that AI, which must draw on preexisting art, is stealing their work. It also devalues the hours of work they put into manually creating stories and images. Furthermore, AI doesn't know anything about cultural norms, biases, diversity, or racism. So when it draws from and uses questionable works, it exaggerates stereotypes even further.

People in favor of AI argue that AI tools borrowing art is no different than human artists being inspired by things that already exist—such as Andy Warhol's *Campbell's Soup Cans* series. Warhol didn't invent soup cans. He used them as a model and created an interpretation of them. AI could also save human artists time and ensure consistent, high-quality work. It could give them more time for self-care and to spend time being creative in other ways.

Cyberpunk: Peach John is about a main character with amnesia in a futuristic urban setting.

In 2024, the publishing company Shueisha launched a temporary service called Manga Plus Universe. AI translation services allowed fans from around the world to post images, reply to discussions, and participate in polls that revolved around fifteen selected manga in Shueisha's online magazine, *Jump Plus*.

Reading About Writing

Many people like reading manga. They even like reading manga about mangaka. *Bakuman*, created by the duo who wrote and illustrated *Death Note*, Tsugumi Ohba and Takeshi Obata, follows two high school boys trying to make it as manga artists. Tatsuki Fujimoto's *Look Back* portrays two aspiring students driven by rivalry and friendship, using a

In its first eighteen days, *Look Back* grossed ¥1 billion, or $6.4 million, in North American theaters.

supernatural theme as a tool of reflection. Other mangaka have written autobiographies about their struggles and successes. Yoshihiro Tatsumi was involved in manga during the medium's post–World War II rise. After several years of high-pressure, backbreaking work, Tatsumi turned to writing his memoir, *A Drifting Life*. It details the politics of both the country and the publishing industry, as well as Japan's struggles to rebuild after a world war.

Naoko Takeuchi, the creator of *Sailor Moon*, shared another part of mangaka life in a short strip called *Princess Naoko Takeuchi Back-to-Work Punch!!* In this autobiographical tale, Takeuchi shows how she met her husband, *Yu Yu Hakusho* and *Hunter x Hunter* creator Yoshihiro Togashi. They first laid eyes on each other at a meeting for *Weekly Shonen Jump* hosted by mangaka Kazushi Hagiwara. The two were introduced by voice actress Megumi Ogata, who has lent her voice to characters in the anime versions of both *Sailor Moon* and *Yu Yu Hakusho*. The two married in 1999, and their officiants were Kotono Mitsuishi, who voices Usagi Tsukino in *Sailor Moon*, and Nozomu Sasaki, who voices Yusuke Urameshi in *Yu Yu Hakusho*. Both mangaka have continued to share details about their lives together through continuing one-shot strips or author's notes in their tankobon volumes.

Follow the Fame

Manga artists are being discovered in new, nontraditional ways, and in all sorts of places. Non-Japanese artists are joining the industry too. Odunze Whyte Oguguo is a Nigerian-born manga artist living in the United States. He founded a successful indie manga company, Saturday AM, and has hundreds of thousands of followers on social media who watch his drawing tutorials.

Peppe, an Italian mangaka now living in Japan, studied the country's culture and language before moving there permanently. When he completed a manga story that he was proud of, he called up a major publishing company and, to his surprise, they set up a meeting. "That meritocratic quality, wherein even if you're unknown, as long as you have talent you can do what you want to do, is something that I personally really admire about Japanese work culture," he said. "Their default is to trust you, and having that trust makes you want to do your best." Peppe's current series, *Mingo*, is about stereotypes foreigners experience while living abroad.

That isn't to say Japanese creators aren't also going viral. Shinn Uchida, also known as @mangalovepaint, began her art career as a mangaka. She won an art competition for *Ultra Jump* magazine. But then, she went down a different path, turning her career into one that's half art, half performance. She paints manga onto walls in front of live audiences. Her story continues with each canvas she completes. Uchida creates art at expos, on buildings, and even virtually. In 2022, she used digital art to transform Times Square in New York City into a huge manga mural.

CHAPTER THREE

Manga's Influence

Manga's influence has been felt in and far outside of Japan's borders. In fact, manga is Japan's most popular cultural export—even bigger than martial arts, food, or fashion. Some mangakas' work is responsible for bringing manga and anime to fans around the world. Others have become story standards that are replicated over and over again. Whether they're considered tropes or classic tales, aspects of manga have shown up in many other forms of entertainment.

A Familiar Story

One of the most well-known tropes in entertainment features a strong-but-gruff hero who feels responsible for a child who needs protection. In turn, the child helps the ronin hero reclaim some of his humanity. *The Mandalorian*, *The Last of Us*, *Logan*, and *Hawkeye* all owe their plots to Kazuo Koike and Goseki Kojima's graphic adult manga *Lone Wolf and Cub*, which was first published in 1970.

Actor Pedro Pascal (*left*) and director Jon Favreau (*right*) attend the London premiere of *The Mandalorian*'s third season in 2023.

The epic tale follows assassin Ittō Ogami and his young son, Daigorō, on a journey for vengeance. It stretched across twenty-eight tankobon volumes and was also turned into six films as well as TV movies, TV shows, video games, and even a board game.

Yu-Gi-Oh! The Movie: Pyramid of Light **includes a scene where the villain transforms to become more powerful.**

Shotaro Ishinomori was discovered by Osamu Tezuka as a young artist and became his protégé. His 1964 series, *Cyborg 009*, featured the first superhero team Japan had ever seen. In 1971, he partnered with the anime production company Toei to create *Kamen Rider.* He designed the super suit and also drew the manga, which ran concurrently with the anime. *Kamen Rider* featured the first henshin hero—a hero who doesn't have powers all the time and has to transform to get them. *Kaiju Girls*, *Yu-Gi-Oh!*, *My Hero Academia*, and *Sailor Moon* all involve henshin heroes.

Kamen Rider is so popular that many manga have made references to it, including *Monthly Girls' Nozaki-kun*, *Dragon Ball Super*, and *One-Punch Man*.

Visual Gags

There are many common tropes that have woven their way into manga. Some, such as fairy tale settings, magical girls, and will-they, won't-they romances, are related to the story's plot. Others are visual tropes or gags. Here are a few of the more common visual tropes:

Snot bubbles: A character who has dozed off might be shown with a big snot bubble coming from their nose.

Sweat drops: A character who is feeling embarrassment, exasperation, or other stress-related feelings might be drawn with a large sweat drop.

Mangaka might also use lines to show the seriousness or severity of a situation, as demonstrated here.

Popping veins: These symbols look a bit like crosses, with four L-shaped lines making each corner. They might be directly on the character's forehead, like a real vein, or appear over their head or in speech bubbles.

Stress lines: Vertical lines over a character's shadowed forehead emphasize moments of stress.

Characters turning chibi: *Chibi* means "cute" in Japanese, and a manga character being shown in a chibi style out of nowhere—with large eyes, small bodies, and big heads—symbolizes many different feelings. Chibi drawings may indicate confusion, a character looking for forgiveness, total relaxation, or comic relief.

Ikki Kajiwara and Chiba Tetsuya's *Ashita no Joe* (*Joe of Tomorrow* or *Tomorrow's Joe*) was first serialized in *Weekly Shonen Jump* in 1968. It is not well-known outside of Japan, but it inspired sports and shonen artists for decades. Joe is not a traditional heroic character. He's a juvenile delinquent who is uninterested in anything except fighting. He has to hit rock bottom before realizing it's time to go forward to chase his dreams of becoming a boxer. The character development and depictions of depression and trauma have been praised for their realism. Instead of a standard hero versus villain/compete-to-be-the-best format, Joe is impacted by each rival he faces, struggling with limitations, weaknesses, and small moments of victory. The best-selling boxing manga *Hajime no Ippo*, winner of the Kondasha Manga Award in 1991, was inspired by *Ashita no Joe*. The series' fight choreography has also inspired other shonen artists, shaping the storylines of influential manga such as *Dragon Ball Z* and *Naruto*. In 2024, Kodansha published a translated English-language version of the original manga.

Manga and Modern Art

Manga has done more than influence other manga. It has also inspired modern art. Because manga can be understood without words, it can walk the line between story and artwork. Takashi Murakami is a contemporary artist who does both. His most popular paintings feature Mr. DOB, a character first introduced in 1996. Murakami's style blends both Japanese and Western animation and uses a Japanese technique dating back to the nineteenth century. Murakami has created Mr. DOB paintings, sculptures, and even luxury

Stories of Wisdom

Manga has influenced many stories and works of art. But it has taken inspiration from other things too. References to Japanese folklore, cultural events, or important objects show up in many manga storylines. Shinto and Buddhism are the two most popular religions in Japan and have played the biggest roles in shaping its literature. Kami are Shinto spirits that often show up in manga. One of the most popular are kitsune, or fox spirits. *Naruto*, *Yu Yu Hakusho*, and *InuYasha* all feature fox spirits. *The Fox & the Little Tanuki* and *Tamamo-Chan's a Fox!* are manga with fox spirits as main characters.

Miko, or shrine maidens, are another Shinto element often found in manga. Kikyou and Kaede in *InuYasha* are possibly the most well-known examples, but *A Couple of Cuckoos*, *Fushigi Yuugi*, and *Kamisama Kiss* all have shrine maidens who serve as caretakers to Shinto shrines too.

Manga such as *BLEACH* lean heavily on Buddhist elements. Reincarnation and divine beings granting wishes and wisdom are a huge part of the story, and as characters gain powers, they more closely resemble Buddhist deities. Osamu Tezuka wrote *Buddha* in 1972 to tell the story of Siddhartha Gautama, the man who would become Buddha. Although many considered it to be a masterpiece, some took issue with the dramatizations and interpretations of some aspects.

Many kitsune in manga have both an animal and human form.

Murakami was the first Japanese artist to have an exhibit at the Palace of Versailles in France.

handbags. A Mr. DOB print sold in 2010 for two million dollars. Murakami has also created smaller statues using an anime style. In addition, Murakami has published manga stories, designed album covers, and directed music videos.

Shojo Style

Shojo manga and fashion have been tightly intertwined since World War II. Fashion magazines in Japan used manga as inspiration and references for readers who wanted to make their own clothing. At the same time, many shojo manga

Many people around the world accessorize themselves with their favorite characters. As of 2022, *Hello Kitty* had sold more than $84.5 billion worth of accessories worldwide.

artists found the drawings in fashion magazines aesthetically pleasing and referenced them in turn in their manga work. Girls' magazines, aside from focusing on quality stories, emphasized good fashion. They featured full-body shots of manga characters outside page panels or on story covers so readers could see the characters' full outfits. Giveaway prizes were often real-life versions of those clothing items. Small freebies inside manga magazines called *furoku* included paper crafts, fashion accessories, makeup, or bags.

In the 1990s, manga magazines began publishing stories about fashion and style. *Jelly Beans*, *Paradise Kiss*, *Boys Run the Riot*, and *Smile Down the Runway* are all focused around dreams of becoming fashion designers or models. Some publishers even released their own fashion magazines.

By the late 2000s, manga had entered the world of high fashion. *Vogue Japan* wrote about the global obsession with manga style. Prada, Louis Vuitton, Gucci, and others have borrowed manga art for their collections. In 2020, Italian luxury brand Moschino showed off designer Jeremy Scott's Anime Antoinette show. He used designs from Riyoko Ikeda's manga *The Rose of Versailles*. That same year, Balenciaga models walked down the runway carrying *Hello Kitty* handbags, and a few months later, Gucci dedicated a collection to *Doraemon*.

Cosplay

Cosplay changed the way magazines and mangaka saw manga art. Shojo manga especially was drawn to appeal to readers interested in fashion and aesthetics. But mangaka also considered looks that could be easily turned into casual wear or cosplay style. One notable example is *Sailor Moon*, which was first published in 1991. Author Naoko Takeuchi was often inspired by high fashion, and her character art followed the trends of the time, with high-waisted, pleated skirts; big bows; oversized sweaters; denim; and pastel colors.

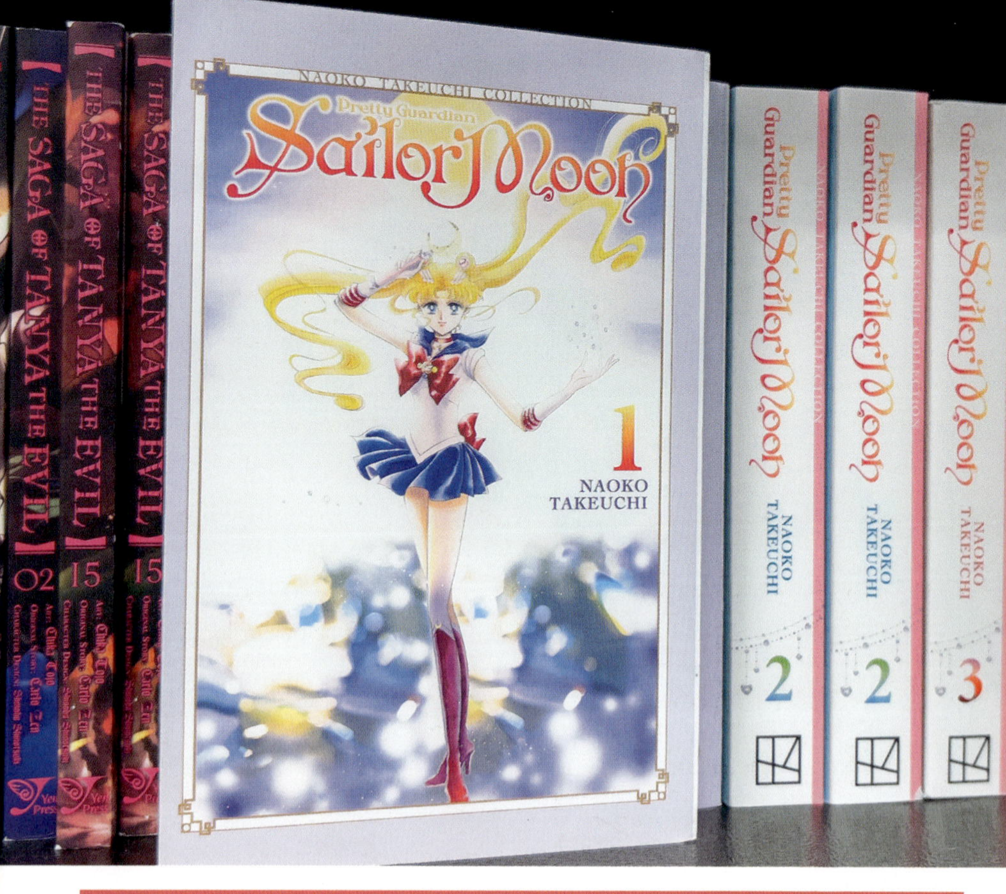

Usagi Tsukino is the main character of *Sailor Moon*. Her magical girl outfit is based on school sailor uniforms.

She showed her readers that heroes could be powerful *and* look good while doing it. *Sailor Moon*'s style was easy for fans to recreate and was also instantly recognizable. Even though it's more than three decades old, *Sailor Moon*'s look continues to inspire high fashion designers such as Gucci and makeup companies such as ColourPop, and it has even shown up in places such as the Olympics.

Cosplay Creators

Cosplay has always been a huge part of manga and anime. In the late 1970s, people began dressing up as their favorite characters. In 1984, anime writer Nobuyuki Takahashi attended a sci-fi convention in Los Angeles, California. He saw people wearing elaborate costumes and coined *cosplay* as a combination of the words *costume* and *play* (or *role-play*). Takahashi went back to Japan and told his readers about it. It didn't take Japanese fans long to add cosplay to their own lives.

Some manga characters are more popular than others to cosplay. With their distinctive clothing and unique details, *Demon Slayer* characters are often at the top of the list. Characters from *My Hero Academia*, *Attack on Titan*, and *Naruto* are also frequently sighted at conventions. Many also draw cosplay ideas from classic manga including *Sailor Moon* and *Dragon Ball Z*. Cosplayers may dress up casually, or they may spend thousands of dollars and take many months collecting or creating the ultimate outfit. Many of the top cosplayers also take commissions to create costumes or pieces for others as a way to fund their hobby.

Cosplayers can participate in formal competitions at conventions or informally get together with other cosplayers.

CHAPTER FOUR

Expand Your Library

It can seem daunting to choose a favorite manga, whether you're a longtime fan or a new convert. There are the old-school, familiar tales that inspired the rest, there are the ones everyone knows, and there are new series just waiting to be discovered. Some are lengthy, taking up tons of shelf space at the bookstore or the library. Others are short but well written, with thoughtful stories and engaging characters. But every list is worth exploring. Here are a few!

CLASSICS: They're called classics for a reason. They've been around for a long time, and they've changed the way people read, understand, and enjoy manga:

Detective Conan, *Fist of the North Star*, *Astro Boy*, *Sailor Moon*

MAINSTREAM: You've probably seen the anime adaptations of these on TV or while scrolling through streaming services. They're so popular that you can get shirts or other merchandise with their characters at places as common as mall department stores:

Fullmetal Alchemist, *InuYasha*, *Black Butler*, *Naruto*, *Attack on Titan*, *Trigun*

Some long-running manga can range anywhere from a few dozen to a few hundred volumes.

HISTORICAL: Take a step through time with a historical manga. These stories take place in the past, with an emphasis on accuracy:

Song of the Long March, *Vinland Saga*, *Kingdom*, *Descending Stories: Showa Genroku Rakugo Shinju*

ALL THE TIME IN THE WORLD: Do you have lots of time to read? These are thousands of chapters long—and when you're done, you can watch the anime version:

JoJo's Bizarre Adventure, *ONE PIECE*, *Sazae-san*, *Kochikame*

ROMANTIC: If you dream of a fairy-tale ending, these manga set up a happily-ever-after for both their characters and their readers:

Strawberry 100%, *Maid Sama!*, *Wotakoi: Love Is Hard for Otaku*, *The Ice Guy and His Cool Female Colleague*, *Wake Up, Sleeping Beauty*, *We Never Learn*

SUPERNATURAL: Aliens? Monsters? Psychic powers? Buckle up because these stories are about to get wild:

Jujutsu Kaisen, *Tokyo Ghoul*, *Toilet-Bound Hanako-kun*, *Mob Psycho 100*

ON THE BIG SCREEN: Grab some buttery popcorn and a sweet treat and get comfortable. Read now, watch later:

Nausicaä of the Valley of the Wind, *Demon Slayer: Kimetsu no Yaiba*, *Ghost in the Shell*, *Akira*

CUTE: Felt cute, might read later. These manga will help cheer you up and dream of a life in a shojo high school:

Ouran High School Host Club, *Love Hina*, *Sailor Moon*, *Skip Beat!*, *Chi's Sweet Home*

SPORTS: Even if you're not a sports fan, these manga will make you feel like you're part of a team:

Haikyu!!, *Slam Dunk*, *The Prince of Tennis*, *Ace of the Diamond*, *Dokaben*, *Medalist*

Read About It

There are many different places to read manga. Bookstores and convenience stores in Japan sell a wide variety of books and magazines. Apps let people discover a new favorite series. Manga cafés offer a quiet place for people to read manga while relaxing, enjoying a warm beverage, or even staying the night. Mandrake was once a pre-owned manga dealer. In 2024, the shop was one of the largest manga and anime stores in the world.

Meiji University in Tokyo opened a manga-specific library in 2009. The school had been gifted a private manga collection belonging to a former rental bookstore owner. He had started a personal collection in 1978 and donated it in 2009. A second large collection belonging to a manga

Manga can be found at specialty bookshops, mainstream bookstores, second-hand and thrift stores, and local libraries.

critic joined it, creating a total collection of around 410,000 volumes of manga spanning five decades. Another large manga library opened in a former school building in Naka, Japan. There are more than 300,000 books available.

For non-Japanese readers, Ohio State University has one of the world's largest collections abroad. It was founded in the mid-1980s by Japanese Studies librarian Maureen Donovan and has been growing ever since. The library now has more than 30,000 volumes of manga and manga-related materials.

The Publishers

There are many manga publishers in Japan, and even more beyond the country's borders. They publish popular series, discover new talent, work with animation companies, and explore additional ways to expand the manga industry.

The biggest publisher in Japan is Shueisha. It was founded in 1925. Shueisha publishes *Weekly Shonen Jump* in both Japan and overseas in more than eighty countries and regions. It also owns VIZ Media, an entertainment company in North America, and has a manga app called MANGA Plus by SHUEISHA. They publish popular manga such as *ONE PIECE, Jujutsu Kaisen*, *Naruto*, and *Demon Slayer*. Other popular series include *Hakutaku*, *Doron Dororon*, *Red Cat Ramen*, and *OSHI NO KO*.

Kodansha is another big publishing company. It's been around since 1909 and is involved with manga production as well as anime, TV dramas, stage plays, and even language textbooks. Its most popular manga magazine is *Weekly Shonen Magazine*. Well-known Kodansha manga include *Witch Hat Atelier*, *Attack on Titan*, *Vinland Saga*, *Fairy Tail*, and *Blue Lock*.

TOKYOPOP is an American publisher. It was founded in 1997 and brought manga to North America. It publishes anime as well as manga, light novels, Western-style manga, and manhwa. It also has a German branch and works with the Walt Disney Company. In 2017, TOKYOPOP established International Women of Manga, which spotlights manga created by diverse women around the world.

Dark Horse was founded in 1986. The next year, it published its first manga: *Godzilla: King of the Monsters*. Founder Mike Richardson was able to cultivate relationships in Japan that led to Dark Horse bringing North American readers *Astro Boy*, *Akira*, *Ghost in the Shell*, *Trigun*, and *Oh My Goddess!*, America's longest-running manga series.

The popular *OSHI NO KO* was published from 2020 until 2024 and was adapted as an anime series in 2023. The series tackles themes such as child stardom and fame, grief and trauma, and the concept of reincarnation.

CHAPTER FIVE

Manga Around the World

Manga is popular around the world. Although around 85 percent of manga was purchased within Asia in 2023, France and the United States are starting to catch up. In fact, France is the second-biggest consumer of manga, with half of all comics bought in France being manga. Other countries recognizing manga's quality is huge for the medium—and Japan recognizing that manga can be made by foreigners is equally as important.

Awarding Talent

In 2007, Japan's foreign minister Taro Aso helped launch the International MANGA Award to spread Japanese culture and encourage international manga artists to try their best. Submissions were judged by a panel of Japanese manga artists, and winners were flown to Japan to meet with other artists and publishers. The first winner was Chinese artist Lee Chi Ching, who was chosen over 145 other entries from twenty-six countries. The levels of awards have been

Although still rare, mangaka outside of Japan are becoming more common.

changed over the years, ranging from ranks—gold, silver, and bronze—as well as additional awards, such as the Commendation Award and the Special Encouragement Award. Winners have been chosen from countries including Saudi Arabia, China, Belgium, Rwanda, Malaysia, Canada, the United States, and France. Some notable works include the following:

I Kill Giants by American writer Joe Kelly and Spanish-Japanese illustrator JM Ken Niimura won the Gold Award in 2012. It was originally published by American publisher Image Comics in 2008. It was published in the seinen magazine *Monthly Ikki* the following year. A coming-of-age tale featuring a girl battling both real and imaginary monsters, the story was turned into a movie in 2017.

Bumbardai by Mongolian creator N. Erdenebayer won the Gold Award in 2015. The story introduces readers to Bumbardai, a five-year-old boy living a nomadic lifestyle.

Malaysian artist Benny Wong (*right*) took runner-up in Japan's first International MANGA Award in 2007.

In 2017, Erdenebayer signed an international publishing contract that would get the series into markets around the world.

Spectrum by Saudi Arabian creator Samah Kamil won the Special Encouragement Award in 2024. Kamil was the first person to receive a master's degree in manga from King Abdulaziz University in Saudi Arabia. There were 587 entries from eighty-two countries that year. Kamil's story is about a girl named Lina who is followed by a strange creature that no one else sees. The monster's presence leads to Lina being diagnosed with autism spectrum disorder.

People Love Manga!

Manga is appealing both to the eyes and to the brain. Following a story through words and pictures helps readers feel like they're part of the world they're reading about. Black-and-white pictures make it easier to follow as well. Manga has made a huge impact on the world of art, literature, and storytelling.

In South Korea, comics are called manhwa and are usually in full color and read as webtoons. In China, they are called manhua and are also colored. And in France, they're called manfra! Each shares similarities and differences with manga, and each works to encourage readers to pick up and enjoy illustrated stories. People in Germany celebrate Manga Day on August 27 every year. Artists in countries such as Senegal, Kenya, and Nigeria are creating stories that tell African history and lore using manga as inspiration. Art collectors are spending millions of dollars on original manga sketches and prints. And manga only continues to get bigger!

Shared Spaces

Some countries find manga competing against their homegrown works. In France, home of the popular hero Asterix, readers bought more than thirty-nine million volumes of manga in 2023. It is the second-largest manga market outside of Japan. Initially, the allure of manga frightened European booksellers. Would *Asterix* and other European comics, such as Belgium's *Tintin*, be lost in favor of manga? But today, the Angoulême International Comics Festival is the third-largest in the world, bringing in more than 200,000 comics and manga fans. There's plenty of room to love comics in all formats.

Manga in America

In North America, creators of all kinds are influenced by manga. Comics done in the "manga style" are easy to recognize by their large eyes and expressive characters and are often labeled as such. *Teen Titans* and *Steven Universe* are two examples of American works inspired by manga. But sometimes these works can lead to confusion among fans and even accusations of appropriation as a result of publishers wanting to jump onto popular trends without fully understanding them.

Some argue that manga is not a style or a genre, so calling something "manga-inspired" is like calling a pop song "music-inspired" or a painting "art-inspired." But others argue that many American cartoonists found inspiration in manga, just as many manga artists found inspiration in

Many mangaka will intentionally arrange their panels to convey information, drum up excitement, or showcase action.

American works. And borrowing manga techniques or styles, such as sticking with black-and-white stories, exaggerated physical features, or highly detailed backgrounds, has been done for decades without diminishing either manga or comics.

The Eisner Awards

Winning a Will Eisner Comic Industry Award, commonly shortened to Eisner Award, is a prestigious achievement in the United States. Likened to the Oscars, this awards ceremony is held at San Diego Comic-Con every year. Will Eisner was one of the first cartoonists in America. Being awarded an Eisner is the biggest honor in comics. The first awards were given in 1988 to works published the previous year. In 2024, there were thirty-two different categories.

Starting in 1998, works could win the Eisner for Best US Edition of International Material. This is an award given to comics not originally published in the US. In 2007, it split into two new categories, with one called Best US Edition of International Material—Japan. This gave non-Japanese works more of a shot, due to how frequently Japanese creators had won the award. (A non-Japanese comic did not win until 2003, and only one non-Japanese Asian novel has ever been given the honor.) Manga has also been nominated in other categories, such as Best Anthology and Best Continuing Series.

Despite Japanese domination in the International Material category for manga, the creators themselves are not as well represented. Junji Ito, author of classics such as *Uzumaki* and *Tomie*, was the first—and only—mangaka to ever win Best Writer/Artist, in 2021. But several have been inducted into the Will Eisner Award Hall of Fame. The first was Osamu Tezuka in 2002. Keiji Nakazawa was recently inducted in 2024. His manga *Barefoot Gen* is based on his experiences as a child living through the Hiroshima bombing. It has been translated into more than twenty languages. Inductees are chosen both by a panel of judges and fans and can be living or deceased. Candidates must have had their first major work published at least thirty-five years prior. The judges' selections may include important contributors who have been overlooked by voters, who have been nominated multiple times, and who were pioneers in the field. The 2023 Hall of Fame class was the biggest in history, with nineteen new inductees.

Eisner Award winners pose together at San Diego Comic-Con in 2023.

Teen Titans Go! shares many similarities with anime, including big eyes and colorful hair.

Learning in the Library

In 2023, *Library Journal* and *School Library Journal* released survey results that showed that teen library readers in the United States love manga. Every public and high school library surveyed has a graphic novel collection, and more than 90 percent of those libraries have a dedicated manga section. Librarians are also recommending manga and graphic novels to readers who aren't connecting with regular books.

Higher education is embracing manga too. Colleges and universities around the world are offering classes—or even degrees—in manga and Japanese art and literature. Kyoto Seika University in Japan offers both undergraduate and advanced degrees in manga.

One influential American creator is Stan Sakai. A third-generation Japanese American, he was raised in Hawaii and grew up watching samurai movies. He got his start in the comic book industry. His most famous work, the still-ongoing series *Usagi Yojimbo*, was first published in 1984. The story follows a samurai rabbit in seventeenth-century Japan. Sakai's goal is to educate people about Japanese history and culture, and he does great amounts of research to make that possible. An animated series based on the Usagi universe, *Samurai Rabbit: The Usagi Chronicles*, came out in 2022 on Netflix. Sakai has received many awards for his work, including a Cultural Ambassador Award from the Japanese American National Museum in 2011. In 2020, he was inducted into the Will Eisner Award Hall of Fame.

Aaron McGruder is another American creator heavily inspired by manga and anime. His syndicated comic strip for adults, *The Boondocks*, ran from 1996 to 2006 and followed the Freemans, a Black family from Chicago living in a white suburban neighborhood. McGruder originally saw *The Boondocks* as a cartoon for grown-ups but realized it would be easier to sell the idea to networks if it was a strip first. Some people have called *The Boondocks* the first Black anime.

Aaron McGruder (*left*) poses with Regina King, who voices both Huey and Riley Freeman in *The Boondocks*.

In 2024, the first American Manga Awards ceremony was held in New York City. Anime NYC and the Japan Society, a cultural organization, partnered to celebrate achievements in the world of manga. Six main awards were handed out that night, including Best New Manga for *#DRCL midnight children* and Best Continuing Manga Series for *Delicious in Dungeon*. *Neighborhood Story* was named the Best New Edition of Classic Manga, and *My Name Is Shingo* took home Best Publication Design. *Witch Hat Atelier* won both Best Translation and Best Lettering.

VIZ published three of the winners; Kodansha, two; and Yen Press, one. Additionally, Frederik L. Schodt was the first person inducted into the Manga Publishing Hall of Fame. He wrote *Manga! Manga! The World of Japanese Comics.* Published in 1983, it was the first substantial English-language resource on the subject.

Manga is helping Japan thrive. It's also getting easier for people around the world to find. Manga is traditionally sold in inexpensive weekly or monthly magazines, but those numbers are trending downward, and sales of tankobon and digital versions are going up. There are also a wider range of tools for new mangaka to create with and more places for them to share with new audiences. Good translations are key when it comes to exporting manga out of Japan. Engaging art and easy ways to obtain manga will draw new fans in, but good writing—and translations—will keep them reading.

CONCLUSION

The Last Chapter

The nearly $14-billion manga industry is estimated to grow by 18 percent between 2024 and 2030. Adults make up a little more than half of manga purchases, but the kids' section is projected to have higher growth—mostly thanks to anime and other manga-adjacent content.

Manga, already on an upward trend, got a huge spike during the COVID-19 pandemic when people were stuck at home looking for new ways to stay busy. In 2020, 10.8 million volumes of manga were sold in the United States, but that number jumped to 27.7 million in 2021, and to 29.6 million in 2022. Although the number dropped to 21.8 million in 2023, its drop was not as extreme as other types of books, and online readers continued to increase.

Funnily enough, there was one singular manga that bucked the trend of digital books outselling physical versions: *ONE PIECE*. Volume 103, which was released in the United States in 2023, was the best-selling volume of *ONE PIECE* that year, selling 71,000 copies. (It had come out in Japan in 2022, where more than three million more volumes of the series were sold that year than the year prior.) The launch of the Netflix live-action anime in 2023 helped drive sales of the manga.

Manga's Tomorrow

Some worry that the modern manga world is shrinking. Being a mangaka is hard work, and the industry is famous for overworking and underpaying. More successful mangaka can hire teams of people to help with smaller tasks such as inking and lettering. Even then, some believe working as part of a huge production group can limit creativity. Mangaka retain control of their creative works but have very little time to spend on being creative. But with an increasingly digital world, there are more tools mangaka can use to streamline their creation process and get their finished stories published.

The more you know about manga, the more you can appreciate it and share that love with others. It may even inspire you to create your own. Manga is no particular type of storytelling or illustration style. It can be whatever you put down on the page. Hone your skills, settle on a story, and get creating!

Manga fans can't get enough of their favorite series!

GLOSSARY

aesthetic: anything that deals with beauty, art, and style

amateur: someone who engages in an activity as a hobby

appropriation: the act of taking something for one's own use, usually without permission

bias: unfair prejudice in favor of (or against) a person, thing, or group

commendation: a formal statement of praise for someone

convention: a gathering of people with similar interests

cosplay: dressing up as a character from a movie, show, book, or video game

ethics: accepted beliefs in what is right and wrong

export: to send something of value to another place

indie: a small company that is not owned by a larger company

induct: to admit someone formally to a position or organization

medium: the material used to create art

memoir: a historical account or biography written by someone who was there

meritocratic: a system where a person's success or power is related to their abilities

net worth: the value of all assets after all taxes and fees are paid

protégé: a person who is guided and supported by an older, more experienced or more influential person

seinen: manga or anime whose primary audience is older men

shojo: manga or anime whose primary audience is young girls

shonen: manga or anime whose primary audience is young boys

stereotype: a generalization or belief about a group of people that is often wrong or biased

storyboard: a sequence of drawings or sketches that helps plan shots for a movie, TV show, or longer story

trope: an overused theme or device

webtoon: a cartoon or series of comic strips published online and read vertically

zine: a small, self-published magazine

SOURCE NOTES

5 "In the past . . . existed until now!": Erik Ko, quoted in Deb Aoki, "Manga Is Booming," *Publisher's Weekly*, April 29, 2022, https://www.publishersweekly.com/pw/by-topic/industry-news/publisher-news/article/89184-manga-is-booming.html.

9 "Many weekly manga . . . on inking it.": Nao Yazawa, quoted in Lisa Wallin, "A Day in the Life of a Manga Artist," *Tokyo Weekender*, June 8, 2018, https://www.tokyoweekender.com/art_and_culture/arts/a-day-in-the-life-of-a-manga-artist/.

17 "Tezuka was always . . . a long time.": Shigeru Mizuki, quoted in Jonathan Soble, "Shigeru Mizuki, Influential Japanese Cartoonist, Dies at 93," *The New York Times*, December 1, 2015, https://www.nytimes.com/2015/12/02/arts/design/shigeru-mizuki-influential-japanese-cartoonist-dies-at-93.html.

23 "That meritocratic quality . . . do your best.": Peppe, quoted in Yukari Mitsuhashi, "Passion, Persistence and Teamwork: How I Made It in Japan as an Italian Manga Artist," *Kintopia*, translated by Alex Steullet, January 14, 2021, https://kintopia.kintone.com/articles/005904.html.

SELECTED BIBLIOGRAPHY

Fox, Joshua. "20 Best-Selling Manga of All Time." ScreenRant, September 15, 2024. https://screenrant.com/best-selling-manga-of-all-time/.

"Giant Manga Publisher Kodansha Launches Official App 'K MANGA' in Canada, Australia, New Zealand, and Singapore." Business Wire, October 21, 2024. https://www.businesswire.com/news/home/20241016640488/en/Giant-Manga-Publisher-Kodansha-Launches-Official-App-%E2%80%9CK-MANGA%E2%80%9D-in-Canada-Australia-New-Zealand-and-Singapore.

"The History of Manga and Its Origins." Japan Avenue, January 27, 2021. https://japan-avenue.com/blogs/japan/history-of-manga?srsltid=AfmBOoodBOT6Z1Xf9yEFDej921s1wM9w25ngeJNStlOWnlkWZhX_fPMH.

Hon, Jason. "One Piece's Recent 'Mistakes' Prove That the Manga's Long Break is Good News." Screen Rant, October 19, 2024. https://screenrant.com/one-piece-mistakes-errors-prove-manga-break-good-news/.

"Manga Genres and Demographics." The Ohio State University, accessed October 22, 2024, https://library.osu.edu/site/manga/manga-genres/.

FURTHER INFORMATION

Books

Bolte, Mari. *The Making of Anime and Manga: From Zodiac Animal Shifters to Demon Slayers*. Minneapolis: Twenty-First Century Books, 2026.
Learn how your favorite anime and manga are made.

Currie-McGhee, Leanne. *Anime and Manga Fandom*. San Diego: ReferencePoint Press, 2022.
Explore the love manga fans have for Japanese comics and how they get involved in entertainment.

Date, Naoto. *Drawing Manga: Tell Exciting Stories with Amazing Characters and Skillful Compositions*. Tokyo: Tuttle Publishing, 2023.
Learn manga art essentials from professional illustrators.

Kanaya, Shunichiro. *A History of Japan in Manga*. Rutland, VT: Tuttle Publishing, 2022.
Read about the history of Japan told through manga.

Koyama-Richard, Brigitte. *One Thousand Years of Manga*. New York: Thames & Hudson, 2022.
This illustrated history of manga traces the origins of Japan's cultural heritage.

Websites

Book Riot: Where to Get Started Reading Manga and Manhwa
https://bookriot.com/start-reading-manga-and-manhwa/
Get help finding a manga or manhwa to add to your collection.

British Museum: Manga: A Brief History in 12 Works
https://www.britishmuseum.org/blog/manga-brief-history-12-works
Scroll through historic works and learn about the impact they made on modern manga.

Carnegie Library: An Introduction to Manga
https://www.carnegielibrary.org/an-introduction-to-manga/
Learn more about manga's roots and how to get started if you are new to the genre.

Ikigai Box: The History of Manga
https://ikigai-box.com/en/blogs/informations/histoire-mangas?srsltid=AfmBOop5V9cvoVXDc2oIndugSoF_JEj9BnWE1kfTFcHIlL7Epf5VvN2G
The history of manga is long. Ikigai Box breaks it down, from its origins to its economic impact.

Kodansha: Kodansha Is Where Manga Meets
https://kodansha.us/manga-meets
Learn about Kodansha's manga selection, find new favorites, learn about the mangaka, and meet other manga fans.

Pratt Institute: An Extremely Brief History of Manga
https://libguides.pratt.edu/graphicnovels/manga
Find out more about manga, peek into the Pratt Institute's library, and find additional resources to make your own manga.

INDEX

ABOUT THE AUTHOR

Mari Bolte is a Korean-American writer and editor who lives in Minnesota with her family and a zoo of pets. She loves books in all formats, but has a special fondness for manhwa and manga.

PHOTO ACKNOWLEDGMENTS

Image credits: EduBFoto/Shutterstock, p.5; BEHROUZ MEHRI/Getty Images, p. 7; Radheya Photos/Shutterstock, p. 8; Michael H/Getty Images, p. 10; NurPhoto/Getty Images, p. 13; Sofyaaaa/Shutterstock, p. 14; Piero Olios/Polaris/Newscom, p. 17; PHILIP FONG/Getty Images, p. 19; Amanda Alamsyah/Shutterstock, p. 20; The Washington Post/Getty Images, p. 25; WARNER BROS. PICTURES/Newscom, p. 26; Imagine China/Newscom, p. 27; malaya itagaki/Shutterstock, p. 28; Prutamin_C/Shutterstock, p. 30; AFP/Getty Images, p. 31; Jeremy Moeller/Getty Images, p. 32; Colleen Michaels/Shutterstock, p. 34; Roy Rochlin/Getty Images, p. 35; Ernesto R. Ageitos/Getty Images, p. 37; STEPHANE MOUCHMOUCHE/Getty Images, p. 39; Usa-Pyon/Shutterstock, p. 41; VALENTINE CHAPUIS/Getty Images; p. 43; YOSHIKAZU TSUNO/Getty Images, p. 44; M. Faisal Riza/Shutterstock, p. 47; Albert L. Ortega/Getty Images, p. 49; Kathy Hutchins/Shutterstock, p. 50; E. Charbonneau/Getty Images, p. 52; Alantide Phototravel/Getty Images, p. 55.

Cover image: ali gaber/iStock/Getty Images